Letter of the Supreme Pontiff
Pope John Paul II

To All the Bishops
of the Church

THE MYSTERY
AND WORSHIP
OF THE
EUCHARIST

Dominicae Cenae

St. Paul Books & Media

Reprinted with permission from *L'Osservatore Romano,* English Edition.

ISBN 0-8198-4748-8

Printed and published in the U.S.A. by St. Paul Books & Media
50 St. Paul's Avenue, Boston, MA 02130

St. Paul Books & Media is the publishing house of the Daughters of St. Paul,
an international congregation of women religious serving the Church with
the communications media.

CONTENTS

My venerable and dear brothers,

1. Again this year, for Holy Thursday, I am writing a letter to all of you. This letter has an immediate connection with the one which you received last year on the same occasion, together with the letter to the priests. I wish *in the first place to thank you cordially* for having accepted my previous letters with that spirit of unity which the Lord established between us, and also for having transmitted to your priests the thoughts that I desired to express at the beginning of my pontificate.

During the Eucharistic Liturgy of Holy Thursday, you renewed, together with your priests, the promises and commitments undertaken at the moment of ordination. Many of you, venerable and dear brothers, told me about it later, also adding words of personal thanks, and indeed often sending those expressed by your priests. Furthermore, many priests expressed their joy, both because of the profound and solemn character of Holy Thursday as the annual "feast of priests" and also because of the importance of the subjects dealt with in the letter addressed to them.

Those replies form a rich collection which once more indicates how dear to the vast majority of priests of the Catholic Church is the path of the priestly life, the path along which this Church has been journeying for centuries: how much they love and esteem it, and how much they desire to follow it for the future.

At this point I must add that *only a certain number of matters were dealt with in the letter to priests,* as was in fact emphasized at the beginning of the document.[1] Furthermore, the main stress was laid upon the pastoral character of the priestly ministry; but this certainly does not mean that those groups of priests who are not engaged in direct pastoral activity were not also taken into consideration. In this regard I would refer once more to the teaching of the Second Vatican Council, and also to the declarations of the 1971 Synod of Bishops.

The pastoral character of the priestly ministry does not cease to mark the life of every priest, even if the daily tasks that he carries out are not explicitly directed to the pastoral administration of the sacraments. In this sense, the letter written to the priests on Holy Thursday was addressed to them all, without any exception, even though, as I said above, it did not deal with all the aspects of the life and activity of priests. I think this clarification is useful and opportune at the beginning of the present letter:

I. THE EUCHARISTIC MYSTERY IN THE LIFE OF THE CHURCH AND OF THE PRIEST

Eucharist and Priesthood

2. The present letter that I am addressing to you, my venerable and dear brothers in the episcopate— and which is, as I have said, in a certain way a continuation of the previous one—is also closely linked with the mystery of Holy Thursday, and is related to the priesthood. In fact I intend to devote it to the

Eucharist, and in particular *to certain aspects of the Eucharistic Mystery and its impact on the lives of those who are the ministers of It:* and so those to whom this letter is directly addressed are you, the bishops of the Church; together with you, all the priests; and, in their own rank, the deacons too.

In reality, the ministerial and hierarchical priesthood, the priesthood of the bishops and the priests, and, at their side, the ministry of the deacons—ministries which normally begin with the proclamation of the Gospel—are in the closest relationship with the Eucharist. The Eucharist is the principal and central *raison d'être* of the sacrament of the priesthood, which effectively came into being at the moment of the institution of the Eucharist, and together with it.[2] Not without reason the words "Do this in memory of me" are said immediately after the words of eucharistic consecration, and we repeat them every time we celebrate the holy Sacrifice.[3]

Through our ordination—the celebration of which is linked to the holy Mass from the very first liturgical evidence[4]—we are united in a singular and exceptional way to the Eucharist. In a certain way we derive *from* it and exist *for* it. We are also, and in a special way, responsible for it—each priest in his own community and each bishop by virtue of the care of all the communities entrusted to him, on the basis of the *sollicitudo omnium ecclesiarum* that St. Paul speaks of.[5] Thus we bishops and priests are entrusted with the great "mystery of Faith," and while it is also given to the whole People of God, to all believers in Christ, yet to us has been entrusted the Eucharist also "for" others, who expect from us a particular witness of veneration and love towards this sacrament, so that they too may be able to be built up and vivified "to offer spiritual sacrifices."[6]

In this way our eucharistic worship, both in the celebration of Mass and in our devotion to the Blessed Sacrament, is like a life-giving current that links our ministerial or hierarchical priesthood to the common priesthood of the faithful, and presents it in its vertical dimension and with its central value. The priest fulfills his principal mission and is manifested in all his fullness when he celebrates the Eucharist,[7] and this manifestation is more complete when he himself allows the depth of that mystery to become visible, so that it alone shines forth in people's hearts and minds, through his ministry. This is the supreme exercise of the "kingly priesthood," "the source and summit of all Christian life."[8]

Worship of the Eucharistic Mystery

3. This worship is directed towards God the Father through Jesus Christ in the Holy Spirit. In the first place towards the Father, who, as St. John's Gospel says, "loved the world so much that he gave his only Son, so that everyone who believes in him may not be lost but may have eternal life."[9]

It is also directed, in the Holy Spirit, to the incarnate Son, in the economy of salvation, especially at that moment of supreme dedication and total abandonment of Himself to which the words uttered in the Upper Room refer: "This is my body given up for you.... This is the cup of my blood shed for you...."[10] The liturgical acclamation: "We proclaim your death, Lord Jesus" takes us back precisely to that moment; and with the proclamation of His resurrection we embrace in the same act of veneration Christ risen and glorified "at the right hand of the Father," as also the expectation of His "coming in glory." *Yet it is the voluntary emptying of Himself, accepted by the Father*

5

and glorified with the resurrection, which, sacramentally celebrated together with the resurrection, brings us to adore the Redeemer who "became obedient unto death, even death on a cross."[11]

And this adoration of ours contains yet another special characteristic. It is compenetrated by the greatness of that human death, in which the world, that is to say each one of us, has been loved "to the end."[12] Thus it is also a response that tries to repay that love immolated even to the death on the cross: it is our "Eucharist," that is to say our giving Him thanks, our praise of Him for having redeemed us by His death and made us sharers in immortal life through His resurrection.

This worship, given therefore to the Trinity of the Father and of the Son and of the Holy Spirit, above all accompanies and permeates the celebration of the Eucharistic Liturgy. But it must fill our churches also outside the timetable of Masses. Indeed, since the Eucharistic Mystery was instituted out of love, and makes Christ sacramentally present, it is worthy of thanksgiving and worship. And this worship must be prominent in all our encounters with the Blessed Sacrament, both when we visit our churches and when the sacred species are taken to the sick and administered to them.

Adoration of Christ in this sacrament of love must also find expression *in various forms of eucharistic devotion:* personal prayer before the Blessed Sacrament, Hours of Adoration, periods of exposition—short, prolonged and annual (Forty Hours)—eucharistic benediction, eucharistic processions, eucharistic congresses.[13] A particular mention should be made at this point of the Solemnity of the Body and Blood of Christ as an act of public worship rendered to Christ present in the Eucharist, a feast instituted by my predecessor Urban IV in memory of the institution of this great

Mystery.[14] All this therefore corresponds to the general principles and particular norms already long in existence but newly formulated during or after the Second Vatican Council.[15]

The encouragement and the deepening of eucharistic worship are *proofs of that authentic renewal* which the council set itself as an aim and of which they are *the central point*. And this, venerable and dear brothers, deserves separate reflection. The Church and the world have a great need of eucharistic worship. Jesus waits for us in this sacrament of love. Let us be generous with our time in going to meet Him in adoration and in contemplation that is full of faith and ready to make reparation for the great faults and crimes of the world. May our adoration never cease.

Eucharist and Church

4. Thanks to the Council we have realized with renewed force the following truth: Just as the Church "makes the Eucharist" so "the Eucharist builds up" the Church[16]; and this truth is closely bound up with the mystery of Holy Thursday. The Church was founded, as the new community of the People of God, in the apostolic community of those Twelve who, at the Last Supper, became partakers of the body and blood of the Lord under the species of bread and wine. Christ had said to them: "Take and eat.... Take and drink." And carrying out this command of His, they entered for the first time into sacramental communion with the Son of God, a communion that is a pledge of eternal life. From that moment until the end of time, *the Church is being built up through that same communion with the Son of God, a communion which is a pledge of the eternal Passover.*

Dear and venerable brothers in the episcopate, as teachers and custodians of the salvific truth of the Eucharist, we must always and everywhere preserve this meaning and this dimension of the sacramental encounter and intimacy with Christ. It is precisely these elements which constitute the very substance of eucharistic worship. The meaning of the truth expounded above in no way diminishes—in fact, it facilitates—the eucharistic character of spiritual drawing together and union between the people who share in the sacrifice, which then in Communion becomes for them the banquet. This drawing together and this union, the prototype of which is the union of the Apostles about Christ at the Last Supper, express the Church and bring her into being.

But the Church is not brought into being only through the union of people, through the experience of brotherhood to which the Eucharistic Banquet gives rise. The Church is brought into being when, in that fraternal union and communion, we celebrate the sacrifice of the cross of Christ, when we proclaim "the Lord's death until he comes,"[17] and later, when, being deeply compenetrated with the mystery of our salvation, we approach as a community the table of the Lord, in order to be nourished there, in a sacramental manner, by the fruits of the holy Sacrifice of propitiation. Therefore in eucharistic Communion we receive Christ, Christ Himself; and our union with Him, which is a gift and grace for each individual, brings it about that in Him we are also associated in the unity of His body which is the Church.

Only in this way, through that faith and that disposition of mind, is there brought about that building up of the Church, which in the Eucharist truly finds its "source and summit," according to the well-known expression of the Second Vatican Council.[18]

8

This truth, which as a result of the same Council has received a new and vigorous emphasis,[19] must be a frequent theme of our reflection and teaching. Let all pastoral activity be nourished by it, and may it also be food for ourselves and for all the priests who collaborate with us, and likewise for the whole of the communities entrusted to us. In this practice there should thus be revealed, almost at every step, that *close relationship between the Church's spiritual and apostolic vitality* and *the Eucharist, understood in its profound significance* and from all points of view.[20]

Eucharist and Charity

5. Before proceeding to more detailed observations on the subject of the celebration of the holy Sacrifice, I wish briefly to reaffirm the fact that eucharistic worship constitutes the soul of all Christian life. In fact, Christian life is expressed in the fulfilling of the greatest commandment, that is to say, in the love of God and neighbor, and this love finds its source in the Blessed Sacrament, which is commonly called the sacrament of love.

The Eucharist signifies this charity, and therefore recalls it, makes it present *and at the same time brings it about.* Every time that we consciously share in it, there opens in our souls a real dimension of that unfathomable love that includes everything that God has done and continues to do for us human beings, as Christ says: "My Father goes on working, and so do I."[21] Together with this unfathomable and free gift, which is *charity* revealed in its fullest degree in the saving sacrifice of the Son of God, the sacrifice of which the Eucharist is the indelible sign, there also springs up within us a lively response of love. We not only know love; we ourselves *begin to love.* We enter, so to speak, upon the path of love and along this path make progress. Thanks to the Eucharist, the love that springs up within us from the Eucharist develops in us, becomes deeper and grows stronger.

Eucharistic worship is therefore precisely the expression of that love which is the authentic and deepest characteristic of the Christian vocation. This worship springs from the love and serves the love to which we are all called in Jesus Christ.[22] A living fruit of this worship is the perfecting of the image of God that we bear within us, an image that corresponds to the one that Christ has revealed in us. As we thus become adorers of the Father "in spirit and truth,"[23] we mature in an ever fuller union with Christ, we are ever more united to Him, and—if one may use the expression—we are ever more in harmony with Him.

The doctrine of the Eucharist, sign of unity and bond of charity, taught by St. Paul,[24] has been in subsequent times deepened by the writings of very many saints who are living examples for us of Eucharistic worship. We must always have this reality before our eyes, and at the same time we must continually try to bring it about that our own generation too may add new examples to those marvelous examples of the past, new examples no less living and eloquent, that will reflect the age to which we belong.

Eucharist and Neighbor

6. *The authentic sense of the Eucharist becomes of itself the school of active love for neighbor.* We know that this is the true and full order of love that the Lord has taught us: "By this love you have for one another, everyone will know that you are my disciples."[25] The Eucharist educates us to this love in a deeper way; it shows us, in fact, what value each person, our brother

or sister, has in God's eyes, if Christ offers Himself equally to each one, under the species of bread and wine. If our Eucharistic worship is authentic, it must make us grow in awareness of the dignity of each person. The awareness of that dignity becomes the *deepest motive of our relationship with our neighbor.*

We must also become particularly sensitive to all human suffering and misery, to all injustice and wrong, and seek the way to redress them effectively. Let us learn to discover with respect the truth about the inner self that becomes the dwelling place of God present in the Eucharist. Christ comes into the hearts of our brothers and sisters and visits their consciences. How the image of each and every one changes, when we become aware of this reality, when we make it the subject of our reflections! The sense of the Eucharistic Mystery leads us to a love for our neighbor, to a love for every human being.[26]

Eucharist and Life

7. Since therefore the Eucharist is the source of charity, it has always been at the center of the life of Christ's disciples. It has the appearance of bread and wine, that is to say of food and drink; it is therefore as familiar to people, as closely linked to their life, as food and drink. The veneration of God, who is love, springs, in eucharistic worship, from that kind of intimacy in which *He Himself, by analogy with food and drink, fills our spiritual being*, ensuring its life, as food and drink do. This "eucharistic" veneration of God therefore strictly corresponds to His saving plan. He Himself, the Father, wants the "true worshipers"[27] to worship Him precisely in this way, and it is Christ who expresses this desire, both with His words and likewise

with this sacrament in which He makes possible worship of the Father in the way most in conformity with the Father's will.

From this concept of eucharistic worship there then stems the whole *sacramental style of the Christian's life.* In fact, leading a life based on the sacraments and animated by the common priesthood means in the first place that Christians desire God to act in them in order to enable them to attain, in the Spirit, "the fullness of Christ himself."[28] God, on His part, does not touch them only through events and by this inner grace; He also acts in them with greater certainty and power through the sacraments. The sacraments give the lives of Christians a sacramental style.

Now, of all the sacraments it is the Holy Eucharist that brings to fullness their initiation as Christians and confers upon the exercise of the common priesthood that sacramental and ecclesial form that links it—as we mentioned before[29]—to the exercise of the ministerial priesthood. In this way eucharistic worship is the *center and goal of all sacramental life.*[30] In the depths of eucharistic worship we find a continual echo of the sacraments of Christian initiation: Baptism and Confirmation. Where better is there expressed the truth that we are not only "called God's children" but "that is what we are"[31] by virtue of the sacrament of Baptism, if not precisely in the fact that in the Eucharist we become partakers of the body and blood of God's only Son? And what predisposes us more to be "true witnesses of Christ"[32] before the world—as we are enabled to be by the sacrament of Confirmation—than Eucharistic Communion, in which Christ bears witness to us, and we to Him?

It is impossible to analyze here in greater detail the links between the Eucharist and the other sacraments, in particular with the sacrament of family life and the sacrament of the sick. In the encyclical *Redemptor hominis*[33] I have already drawn attention to the close link between the sacrament of Penance and the sacrament of the Eucharist. *It is not only that Penance leads to the Eucharist, but that the Eucharist also leads to Penance.* For when we realize who it is that we receive in Eucharistic Communion, there springs up in us almost spontaneously a sense of unworthiness, together with sorrow for our sins and an interior need for purification.

But we must always take care that this great meeting with Christ in the Eucharist does not become a mere habit, and that we do not receive Him unworthily, that is to say, in a state of mortal sin. The practice of the virtue of penance and the sacrament of Penance are essential for sustaining in us and continually deepening that spirit of veneration which man owes to God Himself and to His love so marvelously revealed. The purpose of these words is to put forward some general reflections on worship of the Eucharistic Mystery, and they could be developed at greater length and more fully. In particular, it would be possible to link what has been said about the effects of the Eucharist on love for others with what we have just noted about commitments undertaken towards humanity and the Church in Eucharistic Communion, and then outline the picture of that "new earth"[34] that springs from the Eucharist through every "new self."[35] *In this sacrament* of bread and wine, of food and drink, *everything that is human really undergoes a singular transformation and elevation.* Eucharistic worship is not so much worship of the inaccessible transcendence as worship of the divine condescension, and it is also the merciful and redeeming transformation of the world in the human heart.

Recalling all this only very briefly, I wish, notwithstanding this brevity, to create a wider context for the questions that I shall subsequently have to deal with: These questions are closely linked with the celebration of the holy Sacrifice. In fact, in that celebration there is expressed in a more direct way the worship of the Eucharist. This worship comes from the heart, as a most precious homage inspired by the faith, hope and charity which were infused into us at Baptism. And it is precisely about this that I wish to write to you in this letter, venerable and dear brothers in the episcopate, and with you to the priests and deacons. It will be followed by detailed indications from the Sacred Congregation for the Sacraments and Divine Worship.

II. THE SACRED CHARACTER OF THE EUCHARIST AND SACRIFICE

Sacred Character

8. Beginning with the Upper Room and Holy Thursday, the celebration of the Eucharist has a long history, a history as long as that of the Church. In the course of this history the secondary elements have undergone certain changes, *but there has been no change in the essence of the "Mysterium"* instituted by the Redeemer of the world at the Last Supper. The Second Vatican Council too brought alterations, as a result of which the present liturgy of the Mass is different in some ways from the one known before the Council. We do not intend to speak of these differences: It is better that we should now concentrate on what is essential and immutable in the Eucharistic Liturgy.

There is a close link between this element of the Eucharist and its sacredness, that is to say, its being a holy and sacred action. Holy and sacred, because in it are the continual presence and action of Christ, "the Holy One" of God,[36] "anointed with the Holy Spirit,"[37] "consecrated by the Father"[38] to lay down His life of His own accord and to take it up again,[39] and the High Priest of the New Covenant.[40] For it is He who, represented by the celebrant, makes His entrance into the sanctuary and proclaims His Gospel. It is He who is "the offerer and the offered, the consecrator and the consecrated."[41] The Eucharist is a holy and sacred action, because it constitutes the sacred species, the *Sancta sanctis*, that is to say, the "holy things (Christ, the Holy One) given to the Holy," as all the Eastern liturgies sing at the moment when the eucharistic Bread is raised in order to invite the faithful to the Lord's Supper.

The sacredness of the Mass, therefore, is not a "sacralization," that is to say, something that man adds to Christ's action in the Upper Room, for the Holy Thursday supper was a sacred rite, a primary and constitutive liturgy, through which Christ, by pledging to give His life for us, Himself celebrated sacramentally the mystery of His passion and resurrection, the heart of every Mass. Our Masses, being derived from this liturgy, possess of themselves a complete liturgical form, which, in spite of its variations in line with the families of rites, remains substantially the same. The sacred character of the Mass is a sacredness instituted by Christ. The words and actions of every priest, answered by the conscious active participation of the whole eucharistic assembly, echo the words and actions of Holy Thursday.

The priest offers the holy Sacrifice *in persona Christi;* this means more than offering "in the name of" or "in place of" Christ. *In persona* means in specific sacramental identification with "the eternal High Priest"[42] who is the author and principal subject of this sacrifice of His, a sacrifice in which, in truth, nobody can take His place. Only He—only Christ—was able and is always able to be the true and effective "expiation for our sins and...for the sins of the whole world."[43] Only His sacrifice—and no one else's—was able and is able to have a "propitiatory power" be fore God, the Trinity, and the transcendent holiness. Awareness of this reality throws a certain light on the character and significance of the priest celebrant who, *by confecting the holy Sacrifice and acting "in persona Christi,"* is sacramentally (and ineffably) brought into that most profound *sacredness*, and made part of it, spiritually linking with it in turn all those participating in the eucharistic assembly.

This sacred rite, which is actuated in different liturgical forms, may lack some secondary elements, but it can in no way lack its essential sacred character and sacramentality, since these are willed by Christ and transmitted and regulated by the Church. Neither can this sacred rite be utilized for other ends. If separated from its distinctive sacrificial and sacramental nature, the Eucharistic Mystery simply ceases to be. It admits of no "profane" imitation, an imitation that would very easily (indeed regularly) become a profanation. This must always be remembered, perhaps above all in our time, when we see a tendency to do away with the distinction between the "sacred" and "profane," given the widespread tendency, at least in some places, to desacralize everything.

In view of this fact, *the Church has a special duty to safeguard and strengthen the sacredness of the Eucharist.* In our pluralistic and often deliberately secularized society, *the living faith* of the Christian community—a faith always aware of its rights vis-à-vis those who do not share that faith—ensures respect for this sacredness. The duty to respect each person's faith is the complement of the natural and civil right to freedom of conscience and of religion.

The sacred character of the Eucharist has found and continues to find expression in the terminology of theology and the liturgy.[44] This sense of the objective sacred character of the Eucharistic Mystery is so much part of the faith of the People of God that their faith is enriched and strengthened by it.[45] Therefore the ministers of the Eucharist must, especially today, be illumined by the fullness of this living faith, and in its light they must understand and perform all that is part, by Christ's will and the will of His Church, of their priestly ministry.

Sacrifice

9. The Eucharist is above all else a sacrifice. It is the sacrifice of the Redemption and also the sacrifice of the New Covenant,[46] as we believe and as the Eastern Churches clearly profess: "Today's sacrifice," the Greek Church stated centuries ago, "is like that offered once by the Only-begotten Incarnate Word; it is offered by Him (now as then), since it is one and the same sacrifice."[47] Accordingly, precisely by making this single sacrifice of our salvation present, man and the world are restored to God through the paschal newness of Redemption. This restoration cannot cease to be: it is the foundation of the "new and eternal covenant" of God with man and of man with God. If it were missing, one would have to question both the excellence of the sacrifice of the Redemption, which in fact was perfect and definitive, and also the sacrificial

value of the Mass. In fact, the Eucharist, being a true sacrifice, brings about this restoration to God.

Consequently, the celebrant, as minister of this sacrifice, is the authentic *priest*, performing—in virtue of the specific power of sacred ordination—a true sacrificial act that brings creation back to God. Although all those who participate in the Eucharist do not confect the sacrifice as He does, they offer with Him, by virtue of the common priesthood, their own *spiritual sacrifices* represented by the bread and wine from the moment of their presentation at the altar. For this liturgical action, which takes a solemn form in almost all liturgies, has a "spiritual value and meaning."[48] The bread and wine become in a sense a symbol of all that the eucharistic assembly brings, on its own part, as an offering to God and offers spiritually.

It is important that this first moment of the Liturgy of the Eucharist in the strict sense should find expression in the attitude of the participants. There is a link between this and the offertory "procession" provided for in the recent liturgical reform[49] and accompanied, in keeping with ancient tradition, by a psalm or song. A certain length of time must be allowed, so that all can become aware of this act, which is given expression at the same time by the words of the celebrant.

Awareness of the act of presenting the offerings should be maintained throughout the Mass. Indeed, it should be brought to fullness at the moment of the consecration and of the anamnesis offering, as is demanded by the fundamental value of the moment of the sacrifice. This is shown by the words of the Eucharistic Prayer said aloud by the priest. It seems worthwhile repeating here some expressions in the third Eucharistic Prayer that show in particular the sacrificial character of the Eucharist and link the offering of our persons with Christ's offering: "Look with favor on your Church's offering, and see the Victim whose death has reconciled us to yourself. Grant that we, who are nourished by his body and blood, may be filled with his Holy Spirit, and become one body, one spirit in Christ. May he make us an everlasting gift to you."

This sacrificial value is expressed earlier in every celebration by the words with which the priest concludes the presentation of the gifts, asking the faithful to pray "that my sacrifice and yours may be acceptable to God, the almighty Father." These words are binding, since they express the character of the entire Eucharistic Liturgy and the fullness of its divine and ecclesial content.

All who participate with faith in the Eucharist become aware that it is a "sacrifice," that is to say, a "consecrated Offering." For the bread and wine presented at the altar and accompanied by the devotion and the spiritual sacrifices of the participants are finally consecrated, so as to become *truly, really and substantially* Christ's own body that is given up and His blood that is shed. Thus, by virtue of the consecration, the species of bread and wine re-present[50] in a sacramental, unbloody manner the bloody propitiatory sacrifice offered by Him on the cross to His Father for the salvation of the world. Indeed, He alone, giving Himself as a propitiatory Victim in an act of supreme surrender and immolation, has reconciled humanity with the Father, solely through His sacrifice, "having cancelled the bond which stood against us."[51]

To this sacrifice, which is renewed in a sacramental form on the altar, the offerings of bread and wine, united with the devotion of the faithful, nevertheless bring their unique contribution, since by means of the consecration by the priest they become sacred species.

19

This is made clear by the way in which the priest acts during the Eucharistic Prayer, especially at the consecration, and when the celebration of the holy Sacrifice and participation in it are accompanied by awareness that "the Teacher is here and is calling for you."[52] This call of the Lord to us through His Sacrifice opens our hearts, so that, purified in the mystery of our Redemption, they may be united to Him in Eucharistic Communion, which confers upon participation at Mass a value that is mature, complete and binding on human life: "The Church's intention is that the faithful not only offer the spotless victim but also learn to offer themselves and daily to be drawn into ever more perfect union, through Christ the Mediator, with the Father and with each other, so that at last God may be all in all."[53]

It is therefore very opportune and necessary to continue to actuate a new and intense education, in order to discover all the richness contained in the new liturgy. Indeed, the liturgical renewal that has taken place since the Second Vatican Council has given, so to speak, greater visibility to *the Eucharistic Sacrifice.* One factor contributing to this is that the words of the Eucharistic Prayer are said aloud by the celebrant, particularly the words of consecration, with the acclamation by the assembly immediately after the elevation.

All this should fill us with joy, but we should also remember that *these changes demand new spiritual awareness and maturity,* both on the part of the celebrant—especially now that he ·celebrates "facing the people"—and by the faithful. Eucharistic worship matures and grows when the words of the Eucharistic Prayer, especially the words of consecration, are spoken with great humility and simplicity, in a worthy and fitting way, which is understandable and in keeping with their holiness; when this essential act of the Eucharistic Liturgy is performed unhurriedly; and when it brings about in us such recollection and devotion that the participants become aware of the greatness of the mystery being accomplished and show it by their attitude.

III. THE TWO TABLES OF THE LORD AND THE COMMON POSSESSION OF THE CHURCH

The Table of the Word of God

10. We are well aware that from the earliest times the celebration of the Eucharist has been linked not only with prayer but also with the reading of Sacred Scripture and with singing by the whole assembly. As a result, it has long been possible to apply to the Mass the comparison, made by the Fathers, with the two tables, at which the Church prepares for her children the word of God and the Eucharist, that is, the bread of the Lord. We must therefore go back to the first part of the sacred mystery, the part that at present is most often called the *Liturgy of the Word*, and devote some attention to it.

The reading of the passages of Sacred Scripture chosen for each day *has been subjected by the Council* to new criteria and requirements.[54] As a result of these norms of the Council a new collection of readings has been made, in which there has been applied to some extent the principle of continuity of texts and the principle of making all the sacred books accessible. The insertion of the Psalms with responses into the liturgy makes the participants familiar with the great wealth of Old Testament prayer and poetry. The fact that these texts are read and sung in the vernacular enables everyone to participate with fuller understanding.

Nevertheless, there are also those people who, having been educated on the basis of the old liturgy in Latin, experience the lack of this "one language," which in all the world was an expression of the unity of the Church and through its dignified character elicited a profound sense of the Eucharistic Mystery. It is therefore necessary to show not only understanding but also full respect towards these sentiments and desires. As far as possible these sentiments and desires are to be accommodated, as is moreover provided for in the new dispositions.[55] The Roman Church has special obligations towards Latin, the splendid language of ancient Rome, and she must manifest them whenever the occasion presents itself.

The possibilities that the post-conciliar renewal has introduced in this respect are indeed often utilized so as to make us *witnesses of and sharers in the authentic celebration of the Word of God.* There is also an increase in the number of people taking an active part in this celebration. Groups of readers and cantors, and still more often choirs of men or women, are being set up and are devoting themselves with great enthusiasm to this aspect. The Word of God, Sacred Scripture, is beginning to take on new life in many Christian communities. The faithful gathered for the liturgy prepare with song for listening to the Gospel, which is proclaimed with the devotion and love due to it.

All this is noted with great esteem and gratitude, but it must not be forgotten that complete renewal makes yet other demands. These demands consist in *a new sense of responsibility towards the Word of God* transmitted through the liturgy in various languages, something that is certainly in keeping with the universality of the Gospel and its purposes. The same sense of responsibility also involves the performance of the corresponding liturgical actions (reading or singing), which must accord with the principles of art. To preserve these actions from all artificiality, they should express such capacity, simplicity and dignity as to highlight the special character of the sacred text, even by the very manner of reading or singing.

Accordingly, these demands, which spring from a new responsibility for the Word of God in the liturgy,[56] go yet deeper and *concern the inner attitude* with which the ministers of the Word perform their function in the liturgical assembly.[57] This responsibility also concerns *the choice of texts. The choice has already been made by the competent ecclesiastical authority, which has also made provision for the cases in which readings more suited to a particular situation may be chosen.*[58] Furthermore, it must always be remembered that only the Word of God can be used for Mass readings. The reading of Scripture cannot be replaced by the reading of other texts, however much they may be endowed with undoubted religious and moral values. On the other hand such texts can be used very profitably in the homily. Indeed the homily is supremely suitable for the use of such texts, provided that their content corresponds to the required conditions, since it is one of the tasks that belong to the nature of the homily to show the points of convergence between revealed divine wisdom and noble human thought seeking the truth by various paths.

The Table of the Bread of the Lord

11. The other table of the Eucharistic Mystery, that of the Bread of the Lord, also requires reflection from the viewpoint of the present-day liturgical re-

newal. This is a question of the greatest importance, since it concerns a special act of living faith, and indeed, as has been attested since the earliest centuries,[59] it is a manifestation of *worship of Christ, who in Eucharistic Communion entrusts Himself to each one of us*, to our hearts, our consciences, our lips and our mouths, in the form of food. Therefore there is special need, with regard to this question, for the watchfulness spoken of by the Gospel, on the part of the pastors who have charge of eucharistic worship and on the part of the People of God, whose "sense of the faith"[60] must be very alert and acute particularly in this area.

I therefore wish to entrust this question to the heart of each one of you, venerable and dear brothers in the episcopate. You must above all make it part of your care for all the churches entrusted to you. I ask this of you in the name of the unity that we have received from the Apostles as our heritage, collegial unity. This unity came to birth, in a sense, at the table of the Bread of the Lord on Holy Thursday. With the help of your brothers in the priesthood, do all you can to *safeguard the sacred dignity of the eucharistic ministry and that deep spirit of Eucharistic Communion* which belongs in a special way to the Church as the People of God, and which is also a particular heritage transmitted to us from the Apostles, by various liturgical traditions, and by unnumbered generations of the faithful, who were often heroic witnesses to Christ, educated in "the school of the cross" (Redemption) and of the Eucharist.

It must be remembered that the Eucharist as the table of the Bread of the Lord is a continuous invitation. This is *shown in the liturgy when the celebrant says: "This is the Lamb of God. Happy are those who are called to his supper"*[61]; it is also shown by the familiar Gospel parable about the guests invited to the marriage banquet.[62] Let us remember that in this parable there are many who excuse themselves from accepting the invitation for various reasons.

Moreover our Catholic communities certainly do not lack people who *could participate* in Eucharistic Communion *and do not*, even though they have no serious sin on their conscience as an obstacle. To tell the truth, this attitude, which in some people is linked with an exaggerated severity, has changed in the present century, though it is still to be found here and there. In fact what one finds most often is not so much a feeling of unworthiness as a certain lack of interior willingness, if one may use this expression, a lack of Eucharistic "hunger" and "thirst," which is also a sign of lack of adequate sensitivity towards the great sacrament of love and a lack of understanding of its nature.

However, we also find in recent years another phenomenon. Sometimes, indeed quite frequently, everybody participating in the eucharistic assembly goes to Communion; and on some such occasions, as experienced pastors confirm, there has not been due care to approach the sacrament of Penance so as to purify one's conscience. This can of course mean that those approaching the Lord's table find nothing on their conscience, according to the objective law of God, to keep them from this sublime and joyful act of being sacramentally united with Christ. But there can also be, at least at times, another idea behind this: the idea of the Mass as *only* a banquet[63] in which one shares by *receiving the body of Christ in order to manifest, above all else, fraternal communion.* It is not hard to add to these reasons a certain human respect and mere "conformity."

This phenomenon demands from us watchful attention and a theological and pastoral analysis guided by a sense of great responsibility. We cannot allow the life of our communities to lose the good quality of sensitiveness of Christian conscience, guided solely by respect for Christ, who, when He is received in the Eucharist, should find in the heart of each of us a worthy abode. This question is closely linked not only with the practice of the sacrament of Penance but also with a correct sense of responsibility for the whole deposit of moral teaching and for the precise distinction between good and evil, a distinction which then becomes for each person sharing in the Eucharist the basis for a correct judgment of self to be made in the depths of the personal conscience. St. Paul's words, "Let a man examine himself,"[64] are well known; this judgment is an indispensable condition for a personal decision whether to approach Eucharistic Communion or to abstain.

Celebration of the Eucharist places before us many other requirements regarding the ministry of the eucharistic table. Some of these requirements concern only priests and deacons, others concern all who participate in the Eucharistic Liturgy. Priests and deacons must remember that the service of the table of the Bread of the Lord imposes on them special obligations which refer in the first place to Christ Himself *present in the Eucharist* and secondly to all who actually participate in the Eucharist or who might do so. With regard to the first, perhaps it will not be superfluous to recall the words of the *Pontificale* which on the day of ordination the bishop addresses to the new priest as he hands to him on the paten and in the chalice the bread and wine offered by the faithful and prepared by the deacon: *"Accipe oblationem plebis sanctae Deo offerendam. Agnosce quod agis, imitare quod tractabis, et vitam tuam mysterio dominicae crucis conforma."*[65] This last admonition made to him by the bishop should remain as one of the most precious norms of his eucharistic ministry.

It is from this admonition that the priest's attitude in handling the bread and wine which have become the body and blood of the Redeemer should draw its inspiration. Thus it is necessary for all of us who are ministers of the Eucharist to examine carefully our actions at the altar, in particular the way in which we handle that food and drink which are the body and blood of the Lord our God in our hands: the way in which we distribute Holy Communion; the way in which we perform the purification.

All these actions have a meaning of their own. Naturally, scrupulosity must be avoided, but God preserve us from behaving in a way that lacks respect, from undue hurry, from an impatience that causes scandal. Over and above our commitment to the evangelical mission, our greatest commitment consists in exercising this mysterious power over the body of the Redeemer, and all that is within us should be decisively ordered to this. We should also always remember that to this ministerial power we have been sacramentally consecrated, that we have been chosen from among men "for the good of men."[66] We especially, the priests of the Latin Church, whose ordination rite added in the course of the centuries the custom of anointing the priest's hands, should think about this.

In some countries *the practice of receiving Communion in the hand* has been introduced. This practice has been requested by individual episcopal conferences and has received approval from the Apostolic See. However, cases of a deplorable lack of respect towards the eucharistic species have been reported, cases which are imputable not only to the individuals guilty of such behavior but also to the pastors of the church who have not been vigilant enough regarding the attitude of the faithful towards the Eucharist. It also happens, on occasion, that the free choice of those who prefer to continue the practice of receiving the Eucharist on the tongue is not taken into account in those places where the distribution of Communion in the hand has been authorized. It is therefore difficult in the context of this present letter not to mention the sad phenomena previously referred to. This is in no way meant to refer to those who, receiving the Lord Jesus in the hand, do so with profound reverence and devotion, in those countries where this practice has been authorized.

But one must not forget the primary office of priests, who have been consecrated by their ordination to represent Christ the Priest: for this reason their hands, like their words and their will, have become the direct instruments of Christ. Through this fact, that is, as ministers of the Holy Eucharist, they have a primary responsibility for the sacred species, because it is a total responsibility: they offer the bread and wine, they consecrate it, and then distribute the sacred species to the participants in the assembly who wish to receive them. Deacons can only bring to the altar the offerings of the faithful and, once they have been consecrated by the priest, distribute them. How eloquent therefore, even if not of ancient custom, is the rite of the anointing of the hands in our Latin ordination, as though precisely for these hands a special grace and power of the Holy Spirit is necessary!

To touch the sacred species and *to distribute them with their own hands* is a privilege of the ordained, one which indicates an active participation *in the ministry of the Eucharist.* It is obvious that the Church can grant this faculty to those who are neither priests nor deacons, as is the case with acolytes in the exercise of their ministry, especially if they are destined for future ordination, or with other lay people who are chosen for this to meet a just need, but always after an adequate preparation.

A Common Possession of the Church

12. We cannot, even for a moment, forget that the Eucharist is a special possession belonging to the whole Church. It is the *greatest gift* in the order of grace and of sacrament that the divine Spouse has offered and unceasingly offers to His spouse. And precisely because it is such a gift, all of us should in a spirit of profound faith let ourselves be guided by a sense of truly Christian responsibility. A gift obliges us ever more profoundly because it speaks to us not so much with the force of a strict right as with the force of personal confidence, and thus—without legal obligations—it calls for *trust and gratitude*. The Eucharist is just such a gift and such a possession. We should remain faithful in every detail to what it expresses in itself and to what it asks of us, namely, thanksgiving.

The Eucharist is a common possession of the whole Church as the sacrament of her unity. And thus the Church has the strict duty to specify everything which concerns participation in it and its celebration. We should therefore act according to the principles laid down by the last Council, which, in the Constitution on the Sacred Liturgy, defined the authorizations and obligations of individual bishops in their dioceses and of the episcopal conferences, given the fact that both act in collegial unity with the Apostolic See.

Furthermore we should follow the directives issued by the various departments of the Holy See in this field: be it in liturgical matters, in the rules established by the liturgical books in what concerns the Eucharistic Mystery,[67] and in the Instructions devoted to this mystery, be it with regard to *communicatio in sacris*, in the norms of the *Directorium de re oecumenica*[68] and in the *Instructio de peculiaribus casibus admittendi alios christianos ad communionem eucharisticam in Ecclesia catholica.*[69] And although at this stage of renewal the possibility of a certain "creative" freedom has been permitted, nevertheless this freedom must strictly respect the requirements of substantial unity. We can follow the path of this pluralism (which arises in part from the introduction itself of the various languages into the liturgy) only as long as the essential characteristics of the celebration of the Eucharist are preserved, and the norms prescribed by the recent liturgical reform are respected.

Indispensable effort is required everywhere to ensure that within the pluralism of eucharistic worship envisioned by the Second Vatican Council the unity of which the Eucharist is the sign and cause is clearly manifested.

This task, over which in the nature of things the Apostolic See must keep careful watch, should be assumed not only by each *episcopal conference* but by every minister of the Eucharist, without exception. Each one should also remember that he is responsible for the common good of the whole Church. The *priest as minister*, as celebrant, as the one who presides over the eucharistic assembly of the faithful, should have a special *sense of the common good of the Church*, which he represents through his ministry, but to which he must also be subordinate, according to a correct discipline of faith. He cannot consider himself a "proprietor" who can make free use of the liturgical text and of the sacred rite as if it were his own property, in such a way as to stamp it with his own arbitrary personal style. At times this latter might seem more effective, and it may better correspond to subjective piety; nevertheless, objectively it is always a betrayal of that union which should find its proper expression in the sacrament of unity.

Every priest who offers the holy Sacrifice should recall that during this Sacrifice it is not *only* he with his community that is praying but the whole Church, which is thus expressing in this sacrament her spiritual unity, among other ways by the use of the approved liturgical text. To call this position "mere insistence on uniformity" would only show ignorance of the objective requirements of authentic unity, and would be a symptom of harmful individualism.

This subordination of the minister, of the celebrant, to the *Mysterium* which has been entrusted to him by the Church for the good of the whole People of God, should also find expression in the observance of the liturgical requirements concerning the celebration of the holy Sacrifice. These refer, for example, to dress, and in particular to the vestments worn by the celebrant. Circumstances have of course existed and continue to exist in which the prescriptions do not oblige. We have been greatly moved when reading books written by priests who had been prisoners in extermination camps, with descriptions of Eucharistic Celebrations without the above-mentioned rules, that is to say, without an altar and without vestments. But although in those conditions this was a proof of heroism and deserved profound admiration, nevertheless in *normal conditions* to ignore the liturgical directives can be interpreted as a lack of respect towards the Eucharist, dictated perhaps by individualism or by an absence of a critical sense concerning current opinions, or by a certain *lack of a spirit of faith.*

Upon all of us who, through the *grace* of God, are ministers of the Eucharist, there weighs a particular responsibility for the ideas and attitudes of our brothers and sisters who have been entrusted to our pastoral care. It is our vocation to nurture, above all by personal example, every healthy manifestation of worship towards Christ present and operative in that sacrament of love. May God preserve us from acting otherwise and weakening that worship by "becoming unaccustomed" to various manifestations and forms of eucharistic worship which express a perhaps "traditional" but healthy piety, and which express above all that "sense of the faith" possessed by the whole People of God, as the Second Vatican Council recalled.[70]

As I bring these considerations to an end, I would like to ask forgiveness—in my own name and in the name of all of you, venerable and dear brothers in the episcopate—for everything which, for whatever reason, through whatever human weakness, impatience or negligence, and also through the at times partial, one-sided and erroneous application of the directives of the Second Vatican Council, may have caused scandal and disturbance concerning the interpretation of the doctrine and the veneration due to this great sacrament. And I pray the Lord Jesus that in the future we may avoid in our manner of dealing with this sacred mystery anything which could weaken or disorient in any way the sense of reverence and love that exists in our faithful people.

May Christ Himself help us to follow the path of true renewal towards that fullness of life and of eucharistic worship whereby the Church is built up in that unity that she already possesses, and which she desires to bring to ever greater perfection for the glory of the living God and for the salvation of all humanity.

Conclusion

13. Permit me, venerable and dear brothers, to end these reflections of mine, which have been restricted to a detailed examination of only a few questions. In undertaking these reflections, I have had

before my eyes all the work carried out by the Second Vatican Council, and have kept in mind Paul VI's Encyclical *Mysterium Fidei,* promulgated during that Council, and all the documents issued after the same Council for the purpose of implementing the post-conciliar liturgical renewal. A very close and organic *bond exists between the renewal of the liturgy and the renewal of the whole life of the Church.*

The Church not only acts but also expresses herself in the liturgy, lives by the liturgy and draws from the liturgy the strength for her life. For this reason liturgical renewal carried out correctly in the spirit of the Second Vatican Council is, in a certain sense, the measure and the condition for putting into effect the teaching of that Council which we wish to accept with profound faith, convinced as we are that by means of this Council the Holy Spirit "has spoken to the Church" the truths and given the indications for carrying out her mission among the people of today and tomorrow.

We shall continue in the future to take special care to promote and follow the renewal of the Church according to the teaching of the Second Vatican Council, *in the spirit of an ever living Tradition.* In fact, to the substance of Tradition properly understood belongs also a correct re-reading of the "signs of the times," which require us to draw from the rich treasure of Revelation "things both new and old."[71] Acting in this spirit, in accordance with this counsel of the Gospel, the Second Vatican Council carried out a providential effort to renew the face of the Church in the sacred liturgy, most often having recourse to what is "ancient," what comes from the heritage of the Fathers and is the expression of the faith and doctrine of a Church which has remained united for so many centuries.

In order to be able to continue in the future to put into practice the directives of the Council in the field of liturgy, and in particular in the field of eucharistic worship, *close collaboration is necessary* between the competent department of the Holy See and each episcopal conference, a collaboration which must be *at the same time vigilant and creative.* We must keep our sights fixed on the greatness of the most holy Mystery and at the same time on spiritual movements and social changes, which are so significant for our times, since they not only sometimes create difficulties but also prepare us for a new way of participating in that great Mystery of Faith.

Above all I wish to emphasize that the problems of the liturgy, and in particular of the Eucharistic Liturgy, must not be *an occasion for dividing Catholics and for threatening the unity of the Church.* This is demanded by an elementary understanding of that sacrament which Christ has left us as the source of spiritual unity. And how could the Eucharist, which in the Church is the *sacramentum pietatis, signum unitatis, vinculum caritatis,*[72] form between us at this time a point of division and a source of distortion of thought and of behavior, instead of being the focal point and constitutive center, which it truly is in its essence, of the unity of the Church herself?

We are all equally indebted to our Redeemer. We should all listen together to that spirit of truth and of love whom He has promised to the Church and who is operative in her. In the name of this truth and of this love, in the name of the crucified Christ and of His Mother, I ask you, and beg you: Let us abandon all opposition and division, and let us all unite in this great mission of salvation which is the price and at the same time the fruit of our redemption. The Apostolic See will continue to do all that is possible to provide the means of ensuring that unity of which we speak. Let everyone avoid anything in his own way of acting which could "grieve the Holy Spirit."[73]

In order that this unity and the constant and systematic collaboration which leads to it may be perseveringly continued, I beg on my knees that, through the intercession of Mary, holy spouse of the Holy Spirit and Mother of the Church, we may all receive the light of the Holy Spirit. And blessing everyone, with all my heart I once more address myself to you, my venerable and dear brothers in the episcopate, with a fraternal greeting and with full trust. In this collegial unity in which we share, let us do all we can to ensure that the Eucharist may become an ever greater source of life and light for the consciences of all our brothers and sisters of all the communities in the universal unity of Christ's Church on earth.

In a spirit of fraternal charity, to you and to all our confreres in the priesthood I cordially impart the apostolic blessing.

From the Vatican, February 24, First Sunday of Lent, in the year 1980, the second of the Pontificate.

Joannes Paulus PP. II

Footnotes

1. Cf. Chapter 2: *AAS* 71 (1979), pp. 395f.
2. Cf. Ecumenical Council of Trent, Session XXII, Can. 2: *Conciliorum Oecumenicorum Decreta*, ed. 3, Bologna 1973, p. 735.
3. Because of this precept of the Lord, an Ethiopian Eucharistic Liturgy recalls that the Apostles "established for us patriarchs, archbishops, priests and deacons to celebrate the ritual of your holy Church": *Anaphora Sancti Athanasii: Prex Eucharistica*, Haenggi-Pahl, Fribourg (Switzerland) 1968, p. 183.
4. Cf. *La Tradition apostolique de saint Hippolyte*, nos. 2-4, ed. Botte, Münster-Westfalen 1963, pp. 5-17.
5. 2 Cor. 11:28.
6. 1 Pt. 2:5.
7. Cf. Second Vatican Council, Dogmatic Constitution on the Church *Lumen gentium*, 28; *AAS* 57 (1965), pp. 33f.; Decree on the Ministry and Life of Priests *Presbyterorum Ordinis*, 2, 5: *AAS* 58 (1966), pp. 993, 998; Decree on the Missionary Activity of the Church *Ad gentes*, 39: *AAS* 58 (1966), p. 986.
8. Second Vatican Ecumenical Council, Dogmatic Constitution on the Church *Lumen gentium*, 11: *AAS* 57 (1965), p. 15.
9. Jn. 3:16. It is interesting to note how these words are taken up by the liturgy of St. John Chrysostom immediately before the words of consecration and introduce the latter: cf. *La divina Liturgia del nostro Padre Giovanni Crisostomo*, Roma-Grottaferrata 1967, pp. 104f.
10. Cf. Mt. 26:26-28; Mk. 14:22-25; Lk. 22:18-20; 1 Cor. 11:23-25; cf. also the Eucharistic Prayers.
11. Phil. 2:8.
12. Jn. 13:1.
13. Cf. John Paul II, Homily in Phoenix Park, Dublin, 7: *AAS* 71 (1979), pp. 1074ff.; Sacred Congregation of Rites, instruction *Eucharisticum mysterium: AAS* 59 (1967), pp. 539-573; *Rituale Romanum, De sacra communione et de cultu Mysterii eucharistici extra Missam*, ed. *typica*, 1973. It should be noted that the value of the worship and the sanctifying power of these forms of devotion to the Eucharist depend not so much upon the forms themselves as upon interior attitudes.
14. Cf. *Bull Trasiturus de hoc mundo* (Aug. 11, 1264): *Aemilii Friedberg, Corpus Iuris Canonici*, Pars II. *Decretalium Collectiones*, Leipzig 1881, pp. 1174-1177; *Studi eucharistici*, VII Centenario della Bolla 'Transiturus,' 1264-1964, Orvieto 1966, pp. 302-317.

15. Cf. Paul VI, encyclical letter *Mysterium Fidei: AAS* 57 (1965), pp. 753-774; Sacred Congregation of Rites, Instruction *Eucharisticum Mysterium: AAS* 59 (1967), pp. 539-573; *Rituale Romanum, De sacra communione et de cultu Mysterii eucharistici extra Missam, ed. typica*, 1973.

16. John Paul II, encyclical letter *Redemptor Hominis*, 20: *AAS* 71 (1979), p. 311; cf. Second Vatican Ecumenical Council, Dogmatic Constitution on the Church, *Lumen gentium*, 11: *AAS* 57 (1965), pp. 15f; also, note 57 to Schema II of the same dogmatic constitution, in *Acta Synodalia Sacrosancti Concilii Oecumenici Vaticani II*, vol. II, periodus 2a, pars I, public session II, pp. 251f.; Paul VI, address at the general audience of September 15, 1965: *Insegnamenti di Paolo VI*, III (1965), p. 103; H. de Lubac, *Méditation sur l'Eglise*, 2 ed., Paris 1963, pp. 129-137.

17. 1 Cor. 11:26.

18. Cf. Second Vatican Ecumenical Council, Dogmatic Constitution on the Church *Lumen gentium*, 11: *AAS* 57 (1965) pp. 15f; Constitution on the Sacred Liturgy *Sacrosanctum Concilium*, 10: *AAS* 56 (1964), p. 102; Decree on the Ministry and Life of Priests, *Presbyterorum Ordinis*, 5: *AAS* 58 (1966), pp. 997f.; Decree on the Bishops' Pastoral Office in the Church *Christus Dominus*, 30: *AAS* 58 (1966), pp. 688f.; Decree on the Church's Missionary Activity, *Ad gentes*, 9: *AAS* 58 (1966), pp. 957f.

19. Cf. Second Vatican Ecumenical Council, Dogmatic Constitution on the Church *Lumen gentium*, 26: *AAS* 57 (1965), pp. 31f.; Decree on Ecumenism *Unitatis Redintegratio*, 15: *AAS* 57 (1965), pp. 101f.

20. This is what the Opening Prayer of Holy Thursday asks for: "We pray that in this Eucharist we may find the fullness of love and life": *Missale Romanum, ed. typica altera* 1975, p. 244; also the communion epiclesis of the Roman Missal: "May all of us who share in the body and blood of Christ be brought together in unity by the Holy Spirit. Lord, remember your Church throughout the world; make us grow in love": Eucharistic Prayer II: *ibid.*, pp. 458f.; Eucharistic Prayer III, p. 463.

21. Jn. 5:17.

22. Cf. Prayer after communion of the Mass for the Twenty-second Sunday in Ordinary Time: "Lord, you renew us at your table with the bread of life. May this food strengthen us in love and help us to serve you in each other": *Missale Romanum, ed. cit.*, p. 361.

23. Jn. 4:23.

24. Cf. 1 Cor. 10:17; commented upon by St. Augustine: *In Evangelium Ioannis* tract. 31, 13; *PL* 35, 1613; also commented upon by the Ecumenical Council of Trent, Session XIII, can. 8; *Conciliorum Oecumenicorum Decreta*, ed. 3, Bologna 1973, p. 697, 7; cf. Second Vatican Ecumenical Council, Dogmatic Constitution on the Church, *Lumen gentium*, 7: *AAS* 57 (1965), p. 9.

25. Jn. 13:35.

26. This is expressed by many prayers of the *Roman Missal:* the Prayer over the Gifts from the Common, "For those who work for the underprivileged"; "May we who celebrate the love of your Son also follow the example of your saints and grow in love for you and for one another": *Missale*

Romanum, ed. cit., p. 721; also the Prayer after Communion of the Mass "For Teachers": "May this holy meal help us to follow the example of your saints by showing in our lives the light of truth and love for our brothers": *ibid.*, p. 723; cf. also the Prayer after Communion of the Mass for the Twenty-second Sunday in Ordinary Time, quoted in note 22.

27. Jn. 4:23.

28. Eph. 4:13.

29. Cf. above, no. 2.

30. Cf. Second Vatican Ecumenical Council, Decree on the Missionary Activity of the Church *Ad gentes*, 9, 12: *AAS* 58 (1966), pp. 958-961f.; Decree on the Ministry and Life of Priests *Presbyterorum Ordinis*, 5: *AAS* 58 (1966), p. 997.

31. 1 Jn. 3:1.

32. Second Vatican Ecumenical Council, Dogmatic Constitution on the Church *Lumen gentium*, 11: *AAS* 57 (1965), p. 15.

33. Cf. no. 20: *AAS* 71 (1979), pp. 313f.

34. 2 Pt. 3:13.

35. Col. 3:10.

36. Lk. 1:34; Jn. 6:69; Acts 3:14; Rev. 3:7.

37. Acts 10:38; Lk. 4:18.

38. Jn. 10:36.

39. Cf. Jn. 10:17.

40. Heb. 3:1; 4:15, etc.

41. As was stated in the ninth-century Byzantine liturgy, according to the most ancient codex, known formerly as *Barberino di San Marco* (Florence), and, now that it is kept in the Vatican Apostolic Library, as *Barberini Greco* 366 f. 8 verso, lines 17-20. This part has been published by F.E. Brightman, *Liturgies Eastern and Western*, I. *Eastern Liturgies*, Oxford 1896, p. 318, 34-35.

42. Opening Prayer of the Second Votive Mass of the Holy Eucharist: *Missale Romanum, ed. cit.*, p. 858.

43. 1 Jn. 2:2; cf. *ibid.*, 4:10.

44. We speak of the *divinum Mysterium*, the *Sanctissimum*, the *Sacrosanctum*, meaning what is *sacred* and *holy* par excellence. For their part, the Eastern churches call the Mass *raza* or *mysterion, hagiasmos, quddasa, qedasse*, that is to say "consecration" par excellence. Furthermore there are the liturgical rites, which, in order to inspire a sense of the sacred, prescribe silence, and standing or kneeling, and likewise professions of faith, and the incensation of the Gospel book, the altar, the celebrant and the sacred species. They even recall the assistance of the angelic beings created to serve the Holy God, i.e., with the *Sanctus* of our Latin churches and the *Trisagion* and *Sancta Sanctis* of the Eastern liturgies.

45. For instance, in the invitation to receive communion, this faith has been so formed as to reveal complementary aspects of the presence of Christ the Holy One: the epiphanic aspect noted by the Byzantines ("Blessed is he who comes in the name of the Lord: The Lord is God and *has appeared to us*": *La divina Liturgia del santo nostro Padre Giovanni Crisostomo*, Roma-Grottaferrata 1967, pp. 136f.); the aspect of relation and union sung of by

the Armenians [Liturgy of St. Ignatius of Antioch: *"Unus Pater sanctus nobiscum, unus Filius sanctus nobiscum, unus Spiritus sanctus nobiscum":* Die Anaphora des heiligen Ignatius von Antiochien, übersetzt von A. Rücker, *Oriens Christianus,* 3ᵃ ser., 5 [1930], p. 76); and the hidden heavenly aspect celebrated by the Chaldeans and Malabars (cf. the antiphonal hymn sung by the priest and the assembly after Communion: F.E. Brightman, *op. cit.,* p. 299.

46. Cf. Second Vatican Ecumenical Council, Constitution on the Sacred Liturgy *Sacrosanctum Concilium,* 2, 47: AAS 56 (1964), pp. 83f.; 113; Dogmatic Constitution on the Church *Lumen gentium,* 3 and 28: AAS 57 (1965), pp. 6, 33f.; Decree on Ecumenism *Unitatis Redintegratio,* 2: AAS 57 (1965), p. 91; Decree on the Ministry and Life of Priests *Presbyterorum Ordinis,* 13: AAS 58 (1966), pp. 1011f., Ecumenical Council of Trent, Session XXII, chap. I and II: *Conciliorum Oecumenicorum Decreta,* ed. 3, Bologna 1973, pp. 732f. especially: *una eademque est hostia, idem nunc offerens sacerdotum ministerio, qui se ipsum tunc in cruce obtulit, sola offerendi ratione diversa (ibid.,* p. 733).

47. *Synodus Constantinopolita adversus Sotericum* (January 1156 and May 1157): Angelo Mai, *Spicilegium romanum,* t. X, Rome 1844, p. 77; *PG* 140, 190; cf. Martin Jugie, Dict. Theol. Cath., t. X, 1338; *Theologia dogmatica christianorum orientalium,* Paris, 1930, pp. 317-320.

48. *Instituto Generalis Missalis Romani,* 49c: *Missale Romanum, ed. cit.,* p. 39; cf. Second Vatican Ecumenical Council, Decree on the Ministry and Life of Priests *Presbyterorum Ordinis,* 5: AAS 58 (1966), pp. 997f.

49. *Ordo Missae cum populo,* 18: *Missale Romanum, ed. cit.,* p. 390.

50. Cf. Ecumenical Council of Trent, Session 22, chap I, *Conciliorum Oecumenicorum Decreta,* ed. 3, Bologna 1973, pp. 732f.

51. Col. 2:14.

52. Jn. 11:28.

53. *Instituto Generalis Missalis Romani,* 55f.: *Missale Romanum, ed. cit.,* p. 40.

54. Cf. Constitution on the Sacred Liturgy *Sacrosanctum Concilium,* 35, 51: AAS 56 (1964), pp. 109, 114.

55. Cf. Sacred Congregation of Rites, Instruction *In edicendis normis,* VI, 17-18; VII, 19-20: AAS 57 (1965), pp. 1012f.; Instruction *Musicam Sacram,* IV, 48: AAS 59 (1967), p. 314; Decree *De Titulo Basilicae Minoris,* II, 8: AAS 60 (1968), p. 538; Sacred Congregation for Divine Worship, Notif. *De Missali Romano, Liturgia Horarum et Calendario,* I, 4: AAS 63 (1971), p. 714.

56. Cf. Paul VI, Apostolic Constitution *Missale Romanum:* "We are fully confident that both priests and faithful will prepare their minds and hearts more devoutly for the Lord's Supper, meditating on the scriptures, nourished day by day with the words of the Lord": AAS 61 (1969), pp. 220f.; *Missale Romanum, ed. cit.,* p. 15.

57. Cf. *Pontificale Romanum. De Institutione Lectorum et Acolythorum,* 4, *ed. typica,* 1972, pp. 19f.

58. Cf. *Instituto Generalis Missalis Romani,* 319-320: *Missale Romanum, ed. cit.,* p. 87.

59. Cf. Fr. J. Dölger, *Das Segnen der Sinne mit der Eucharistie. Eine altchristliche Kommunionsitte: Antike und Christentum*, t. 3 (1932), pp. 231-244; *Das Kultvergehen der Donatistin Lucilla von Karthago. Reliquienkuss vor dem Kuss der Eucharistie, ibid.*, pp. 245-252.

60. Cf. Second Vatican Ecumenical Council, Dogmatic Constitution on the Church *Lumen gentium*, 12, 35; *AAS* 57 (1965), pp. 16, 40.

61. Cf. Jn. 1:29; Rv. 19:9.

62. Cf. Lk. 14:16ff.

63. Cf. *Instituto Generalis Missalis Romani*, 7-8: *Missale Romanum, ed. cit.*, p. 29.

64. 1 Cor. 11:28.

65. *Pontificale Romanum. De Ordinatione Diaconi, Presbyteri et Episcopi, ed. typica*, 1968, p. 93.

66. Heb. 5:1.

67. Sacred Congregation of Rites, Instruction *Eucharisticum Mysterium: AAS* 59 (1967), pp. 539-573; *Rituale Romanum. De sacra communione et de cultu Mysterii eucharistici extra Missam, ed. typica*, 1973; Sacred Congregation for Divine Worship, *Litterae circulares ad Conferentiarum Episcopalium Praesides de precibus eucharisticis: AAS* 65 (1973), pp. 340-347.

68. Nos. 38-63: *AAS* 59 (1967), pp. 586-592.

69. *AAS* 64 (1972), pp. 518-525. Cf. also the *Communicatio* published the following year for the correct application of the above-mentioned Instruction: *AAS* 65 (1973), pp. 616-619.

70. Cf. Second Vatican Ecumenical Council, Dogmatic Constitution on the Church *Lumen gentium*, 12: *AAS* 57 (1965), pp. 16f.

71. Mt. 13:52.

72. Cf. St. Augustine, *In Evangelium Ioannis tract.* 26, 13: *PL* 35, 1612f.

73. Eph. 4:30.

St. Paul Book & Media Centers

ALASKA
750 West 5th Ave., Anchorage, AK 99501 907-272-8183.

CALIFORNIA
3908 Sepulveda Blvd., Culver City, CA 90230 310-397-8676.
1570 Fifth Ave. (at Cedar Street), San Diego, CA 92101 619-232-1442;
   619-232-1443.
46 Geary Street, San Francisco, CA 94108 415-781-5180.

FLORIDA
145 S.W. 107th Ave., Miami, FL 33174 305-559-6715; 305-559-6716.

HAWAII
1143 Bishop Street, Honolulu, HI 96813 808-521-2731.

ILLINOIS
172 North Michigan Ave., Chicago, IL 60601 312-346-4228; 312-346-3240.

LOUISIANA
4403 Veterans Memorial Blvd., Metairie, LA 70006 504-887-7631;
   504-887-0113.

MASSACHUSETTS
50 St. Paul's Ave., Jamaica Plain, Boston, MA 02130 617-522-8911.
Rte. 1, 885 Providence Hwy., Dedham, MA 02026 617-326-5385.

MISSOURI
9804 Watson Rd., St. Louis, MO 63126 314-965-3512; 314-965-3571.

NEW JERSEY
561 U.S. Route 1, Wick Plaza, Edison, NJ 08817 908-572-1200.

NEW YORK
150 East 52nd Street, New York, NY 10022 212-754-1110.
78 Fort Place, Staten Island, NY 10301 718-447-5071; 718-447-5086.

OHIO
2105 Ontario Street (at Prospect Ave.), Cleveland, OH 44115 216-621-9427.

PENNSYLVANIA
214 W. DeKalb Pike, King of Prussia, PA 19406 215-337-1882; 215-337-2077.

SOUTH CAROLINA
243 King Street, Charleston, SC 29401 803-577-0175.

TEXAS
114 Main Plaza, San Antonio, TX 78205 210-224-8101.

VIRGINIA
1025 King Street, Alexandria, VA 22314 703-549-3806.

CANADA
3022 Dufferin Street, Toronto, Ontario, Canada M6B 3T5 416-781-9131.